TO TRUST AGAIN
A Remarriage Preparation Program

Couple's Workbook

by
WILLIAM F. URBINE, D. Min.

ACTA Publications
Chicago, Illinois

TO TRUST AGAIN: A Remarriage Preparation Program
Couple's Workbook
by William F. Urbine, D. Min.

William F. Urbine is the administrative supervisor of the Family Life Bureau of the Diocese of Allentown, Pennsylvania. He is a certified family life educator by the National Council on Family Relations. Mr. Urbine is married and the father of four children, two of them adopted.

The Bible passages used in the Prayer Service are from the New American Bible, copyright © 1986 by the Confraternity of Christian Doctrine, Washington, D.C. All rights reserved.

Edited by Gregory F. Augustine Pierce
Design by John Dylong
Typesetting by LINK Book Development and Production

Copyright © 1990: ACTA Publications
                   5559 W. Howard St.
                   Skokie, IL 60077
                   800-397-2282
                   www.actapublications.com

ISBN: 0-915388-42-1

Printed in the United States of America

TABLE OF CONTENTS

INTRODUCTION

To Trust Again is a program for engaged couples of whom one or both partners have experienced a prior marriage or marriages which ended through the death of a spouse or through divorce and / or annulment. If you are in this situation, you already realize that you bring much pain and hurt, as well as wisdom and hope, to your new relationship. Learning to trust again in an intimate relationship of love presents an entirely different set of obstacles and opportunities from those experienced by never-married couples.

The Couple's Workbook contains a variety of exercises and resources to help you think through and share your thoughts and feelings about remarriage, its meaning and its challenges. Don't merely fill out and exchange these exercises. Their value occurs *after* the exchange, when you begin to probe, share feelings, question, and work to understand each other more deeply.

These exercises are tools designed to

- promote and stimulate dialogue
- deepen mutual understanding
- elicit insights and feelings
  about potentially sensitive areas that might not otherwise be discussed.

For each of the exercises, two copies are provided so that each of you can complete the exercise individually before discussing the results. Other items are resources for you to read and think about together.

This workbook is designed to be used in a comprehensive program that includes group meetings and presentations as described in the *To Trust Again* Leader's Guide. There is also a separate *To Trust Again* Remarriage Inventory available that identifies areas of strengths and weaknesses in your relationship. This workbook can also be used profitably by an individual couple without benefit of an organized program.

The sole purpose of these exercises is to help you take a good, long look at marriage—not just any marriage, but *your* marriage.

DISCOVERING EACH OTHER

A gentle exercise to help elicit important feelings that lovers might wish to discuss.

A

Use this column to answer the following items as directly as you can.

PLEASE WORK ALONE.

B

Now, put yourself in your partner's shoes and jot down the answers you think he/she has written under column A.

1. The reason I love you

2. My strongest quality

3. My greatest weakness

4. My usual means of avoiding conflict

5. My usual means of dealing with conflict

6. My biggest worry

7. A sensitive area in which I can't take criticism

8. My greatest interest and concern other than our relationship

_____ _____

_____ _____

_____ _____

9. My definition of sexual love

_____ _____

_____ _____

_____ _____

10. My greatest fear about our upcoming marriage

_____ _____

_____ _____

_____ _____

11. The biggest adjustment I'll have to make in our first year of marriage

_____ _____

_____ _____

_____ _____

12. What describes us best as a couple

_____ _____

_____ _____

_____ _____

13. The thing I find most difficult (unpleasant, confusing) to talk about

_____ _____

_____ _____

_____ _____

14. Five years from now we will be

_____ _____

_____ _____

_____ _____

15. In discussing my former spouse with you, I feel (if applicable)

_____ _____

_____ _____

_____ _____

16. In discussing your former spouse with you, I feel (if applicable)

_____ _____

_____ _____

_____ _____

After you have completed the exercise, exchange papers with your partner . . . relax and compare them. Talk them over. Do any of his/her answers surprise you? Do you disagree with any of his/her answers? Are any especially interesting or thought-provoking?

DISCOVERING EACH OTHER

A gentle exercise to help elicit important feelings that lovers might wish to discuss.

A

Use this column to answer the following items as directly as you can.

PLEASE WORK ALONE.

B

Now, put yourself in your partner's shoes and jot down the answers you think he/she has written under column A.

1. The reason I love you

2. My strongest quality

3. My greatest weakness

4. My usual means of avoiding conflict

5. My usual means of dealing with conflict

6. My biggest worry

7. A sensitive area in which I can't take criticism

8. My greatest interest and concern other than our relationship

_____   _____
_____   _____
_____   _____

9. My definition of sexual love

_____   _____
_____   _____
_____   _____

10. My greatest fear about our upcoming marriage

_____   _____
_____   _____
_____   _____

11. The biggest adjustment I'll have to make in our first year of marriage

_____   _____
_____   _____
_____   _____

12. What describes us best as a couple

_____   _____
_____   _____
_____   _____

13. The thing I find most difficult (unpleasant, confusing) to talk about

_____   _____
_____   _____
_____   _____

14. Five years from now we will be

_____   _____
_____   _____
_____   _____

15. In discussing my former spouse with you, I feel (if applicable)

_____   _____
_____   _____
_____   _____

16. In discussing your former spouse with you, I feel (if applicable)

_____   _____
_____   _____
_____   _____

After you have completed the exercise, exchange papers with your partner . . . relax and compare them. Talk them over. Do any of his/her answers surprise you? Do you disagree with any of his/her answers? Are any especially interesting or thought-provoking?

IF WE DON'T KNOW WHERE WE COME FROM

This exercise will help you identify the ways of relating inside your families of origin (the family you grew up in) which helped each of you become the person you are today. In addition, you can explore the experience of your prior marriage.

First, answer each of the questions on the left below about the family in which you were raised. Circle one, and only one, of the five dots on each horizontal line under the category that best describes your view of how your family of origin operated. Your choices are ALWAYS, USUALLY, SOMETIMES, SELDOM, NEVER. After you have completed the exercise once, go over the questions and answer them on the right as you experienced your prior marriage(s), if any.

When you have finished, compare your results with your partner's and discuss the areas in which you had definite differences in experience of family. Decide how you would like your new family to function. If you cannot agree now, set time aside to discuss the issue at greater length. It is important for the two of you to agree on a plan to resolve differences in relating that will be workable after you are married.

Family of origin — columns: ALWAYS, USUALLY, SOMETIMES, SELDOM, NEVER

Prior marriage(s) — columns: ALWAYS, USUALLY, SOMETIMES, SELDOM, NEVER

Family of origin					Question	Prior marriage(s)				
•	•	•	•	•	Did your family encourage you to express what you thought?	•	•	•	•	•
•	•	•	•	•	Did your family encourage you to express how you felt?	•	•	•	•	•
•	•	•	•	•	In your family, did people take responsibility for their actions?	•	•	•	•	•
•	•	•	•	•	Did your family encourage the expression of differences of opinions?	•	•	•	•	•
•	•	•	•	•	Were members of your family encouraged to listen closely to each other?	•	•	•	•	•
•	•	•	•	•	Did your family express their emotions openly about death, divorce, or other painful losses?	•	•	•	•	•
•	•	•	•	•	Was it acceptable in your family to express both positive and negative feelings?	•	•	•	•	•
•	•	•	•	•	Was your family supportive of you when you tried new "things"?	•	•	•	•	•
•	•	•	•	•	Were you able to work out conflicts in your family?	•	•	•	•	•
•	•	•	•	•	Did your family allow anger to be expressed constructively?	•	•	•	•	•
•	•	•	•	•	Did your family exhibit a sense of humor?	•	•	•	•	•
•	•	•	•	•	Were your family members sensitive to one another's feelings?	•	•	•	•	•
•	•	•	•	•	Did your family encourage you to basically trust others?	•	•	•	•	•
•	•	•	•	•	Did your family tolerate abusive behavior (verbal, physical, sexual)?	•	•	•	•	•
•	•	•	•	•	Did your family relate to each other with both physical and verbal expressions of affection?	•	•	•	•	•

HOW DO YOU SEE ME?

You are invited to compare your views of yourself with your *fiancée's* view of you. This exercise emphasizes the fact that the image we have of ourselves is *not* necessarily the image that even those near and dear to us have.

A. MAN ABOUT HIMSELF

	VERY	SOMEWHAT	NEUTRAL	SOMEWHAT	VERY	
calm	•	•	•	•	•	excitable
assertive	•	•	•	•	•	passive
reserved	•	•	•	•	•	affectionate
skeptical	•	•	•	•	•	trusting
extroverted	•	•	•	•	•	introverted
self-questioning	•	•	•	•	•	confident
procrastinating	•	•	•	•	•	compulsive
spendthrift	•	•	•	•	•	tightwad
happy-go-lucky	•	•	•	•	•	careful planner
realist	•	•	•	•	•	optimist
detached	•	•	•	•	•	sympathetic
social	•	•	•	•	•	private
serious	•	•	•	•	•	whimsical
relaxed	•	•	•	•	•	eager
critical	•	•	•	•	•	permissive
liberal	•	•	•	•	•	conservative
uncommunicative	•	•	•	•	•	communicative
self-sufficient	•	•	•	•	•	reliant
open	•	•	•	•	•	reticent
forceful	•	•	•	•	•	long-suffering
organized	•	•	•	•	•	disorganized
practical	•	•	•	•	•	dreamer
cautious	•	•	•	•	•	bold

B. MAN ABOUT WOMAN

	VERY	SOMEWHAT	NEUTRAL	SOMEWHAT	VERY	
calm	•	•	•	•	•	excitable
assertive	•	•	•	•	•	passive
reserved	•	•	•	•	•	affectionate
skeptical	•	•	•	•	•	trusting
extroverted	•	•	•	•	•	introverted
self-questioning	•	•	•	•	•	confident
procrastinating	•	•	•	•	•	compulsive
spendthrift	•	•	•	•	•	tightwad
happy-go-lucky	•	•	•	•	•	careful planner
realist	•	•	•	•	•	optimist
detached	•	•	•	•	•	sympathetic
social	•	•	•	•	•	private
serious	•	•	•	•	•	whimsical
relaxed	•	•	•	•	•	eager
critical	•	•	•	•	•	permissive
liberal	•	•	•	•	•	conservative
uncommunicative	•	•	•	•	•	communicative
self-sufficient	•	•	•	•	•	reliant
open	•	•	•	•	•	reticent
forceful	•	•	•	•	•	long-suffering
organized	•	•	•	•	•	disorganized
practical	•	•	•	•	•	dreamer
cautious	•	•	•	•	•	bold

1. Mark list A about yourself by circling one, *and only one,* of the five dots on each horizontal line (each of the five dots is keyed to the words above: very, somewhat, neutral, etc.). Circle one dot you feel most nearly describes your personality, e.g., in the first line it might be "very excitable" or "somewhat calm." Then proceed to the next line.

2. Next, mark list B about *your fiancée* by circling dots which most nearly describe your partner's personality traits.

3. Compare the sheets by holding them side by side. First compare A and D, then compare B and C. Discuss the differences in your perceptions of each other.

IF WE DON'T KNOW WHERE WE COME FROM

This exercise will help you identify the ways of relating inside your families of origin (the family you grew up in) which helped each of you become the person you are today. In addition, you can explore the experience of your prior marriage.

First, answer each of the questions on the left below about the family in which you were raised. Circle one, and only one, of the five dots on each horizontal line under the category that best describes your view of how your family of origin operated. Your choices are ALWAYS, USUALLY, SOMETIMES, SELDOM, NEVER. After you have completed the exercise once, go over the questions and answer them on the right as you experienced your prior marriage(s), if any.

When you have finished, compare your results with your partner's and discuss the areas in which you had definite differences in experience of family. Decide how you would like your new family to function. If you cannot agree now, set time aside to discuss the issue at greater length. It is important for the two of you to agree on a plan to resolve differences in relating that will be workable after you are married.

Family of origin						Prior marriage(s)				
ALWAYS	USUALLY	SOMETIMES	SELDOM	NEVER		ALWAYS	USUALLY	SOMETIMES	SELDOM	NEVER
•	•	•	•	•	Did your family encourage you to express what you thought?	•	•	•	•	•
•	•	•	•	•	Did your family encourage you to express how you felt?	•	•	•	•	•
•	•	•	•	•	In your family, did people take responsibility for their actions?	•	•	•	•	•
•	•	•	•	•	Did your family encourage the expression of differences of opinions?	•	•	•	•	•
•	•	•	•	•	Were members of your family encouraged to listen closely to each other?	•	•	•	•	•
•	•	•	•	•	Did your family express their emotions openly about death, divorce, or other painful losses?	•	•	•	•	•
•	•	•	•	•	Was it acceptable in your family to express both positive and negative feelings?	•	•	•	•	•
•	•	•	•	•	Was your family supportive of you when you tried new "things"?	•	•	•	•	•
•	•	•	•	•	Were you able to work out conflicts in your family?	•	•	•	•	•
•	•	•	•	•	Did your family allow anger to be expressed constructively?	•	•	•	•	•
•	•	•	•	•	Did your family exhibit a sense of humor?	•	•	•	•	•
•	•	•	•	•	Were your family members sensitive to one another's feelings?	•	•	•	•	•
•	•	•	•	•	Did your family encourage you to basically trust others?	•	•	•	•	•
•	•	•	•	•	Did your family tolerate abusive behavior (verbal, physical, sexual)?	•	•	•	•	•
•	•	•	•	•	Did your family relate to each other with both physical and verbal expressions of affection?	•	•	•	•	•

HOW DO YOU SEE ME?

You are invited to compare your views of yourself with your *fiancé's* view of you. This exercise emphasizes the fact that the image we have of ourselves is *not* necessarily the image that even those near and dear to us have.

C. WOMAN ABOUT HERSELF

	VERY	SOMEWHAT	NEUTRAL	SOMEWHAT	VERY	
calm	●	●	●	●	●	excitable
assertive	●	●	●	●	●	passive
reserved	●	●	●	●	●	affectionate
skeptical	●	●	●	●	●	trusting
extroverted	●	●	●	●	●	introverted
self-questioning	●	●	●	●	●	confident
procrastinating	●	●	●	●	●	compulsive
spendthrift	●	●	●	●	●	tightwad
happy-go-lucky	●	●	●	●	●	careful planner
realist	●	●	●	●	●	optimist
detached	●	●	●	●	●	sympathetic
social	●	●	●	●	●	private
serious	●	●	●	●	●	whimsical
relaxed	●	●	●	●	●	eager
critical	●	●	●	●	●	permissive
liberal	●	●	●	●	●	conservative
uncommunicative	●	●	●	●	●	communicative
self-sufficient	●	●	●	●	●	reliant
open	●	●	●	●	●	reticent
forceful	●	●	●	●	●	long-suffering
organized	●	●	●	●	●	disorganized
practical	●	●	●	●	●	dreamer
cautious	●	●	●	●	●	bold

D. WOMAN ABOUT MAN

	VERY	SOMEWHAT	NEUTRAL	SOMEWHAT	VERY	
calm	●	●	●	●	●	excitable
assertive	●	●	●	●	●	passive
reserved	●	●	●	●	●	affectionate
skeptical	●	●	●	●	●	trusting
extroverted	●	●	●	●	●	introverted
self-questioning	●	●	●	●	●	confident
procrastinating	●	●	●	●	●	compulsive
spendthrift	●	●	●	●	●	tightwad
happy-go-lucky	●	●	●	●	●	careful planner
realist	●	●	●	●	●	optimist
detached	●	●	●	●	●	sympathetic
social	●	●	●	●	●	private
serious	●	●	●	●	●	whimsical
relaxed	●	●	●	●	●	eager
critical	●	●	●	●	●	permissive
liberal	●	●	●	●	●	conservative
uncommunicative	●	●	●	●	●	communicative
self-sufficient	●	●	●	●	●	reliant
open	●	●	●	●	●	reticent
forceful	●	●	●	●	●	long-suffering
organized	●	●	●	●	●	disorganized
practical	●	●	●	●	●	dreamer
cautious	●	●	●	●	●	bold

1. Mark list C about yourself by circling one, *and only one,* of the five dots on each horizontal line (each of the five dots is keyed to the words above: very, somewhat, neutral, etc.). Circle one dot you feel most nearly describes your personality, e.g., in the first line it might be "very excitable" or "somewhat calm." Then proceed to the next line.

2. Next, mark list D about *your fiancé* by circling dots which most nearly describe your partner's personality traits.

3. Compare the sheets by holding them side by side. First compare A and D, then compare B and C. Discuss the differences in your perceptions of each other.

FIGHTING FAIR

To presume that you will not argue after you are married is idealistic; it simply is not true. You will argue. Many marital therapists would say that a good conflict is often healthy because it promotes dialogue (couples *talk* with one another) and good communication. For some the experience of conflict in a prior marriage or relationship can make them hesitant to disclose their feelings and hurts, but they must take the risk and argue at times.

However, if arguments are to be fair and fruitful, they should follow certain ground rules. The object of an argument is to solve a problem, not to destroy the other person. Although to avoid conflict at all costs is unhealthy and stifling, to argue without certain positive guidelines can be destructive and disheartening. Here are a few tips.

Ground Rules

- Listen to your partner. Give each other the opportunity to speak and don't dominate the discussion.

- Stick to the issues at hand. Don't dredge up past hurts or problems, whether real or perceived.

- Never refer to your partner's former marriage in anger.

- Always complete the argument. To walk away angry or postpone the discussion indefinitely can cause more problems.

- Don't sling mud and arrows. Avoid name-calling. Use of phrases such as "stupid jerk," "fat slob," "drunken bum," or "lazy lump" only serves to hurt and incite more anger.

- Never threaten to withdraw love or sex.

- Don't use the "silent treatment." Nothing gets solved this way.

- When you are wrong, admit it.

- Don't make a scene. Never deliberately embarrass each other or others by arguing in front of other family members or in public. Keep your arguments private.

- Make up and mean it. Don't be bitter or carry a grudge.

Look over the behaviors listed below that are often used to express or respond to anger or negative feelings. In each case, check if it characterizes you, your new partner, or your former spouse(s), if any.

	ME	YOU	FORMER SPOUSE #1	FORMER SPOUSE #2
Silence				
Blaming				
Yelling				
Pouting				
Sarcasm				
Avoidance				
Appeasement				
Crying				
Threatening				
Physical Violence				

Remember: Differences of opinion, when brought to the forefront in a positive, careful manner, can help you grow. Don't argue to hurt and never go to sleep angry. Always call forth the core love you have for your partner and say goodnight with love in your heart.

To get in touch with your feelings and the manner in which you argue, answer the following questions and share your responses with your partner.

- When I get angry, I tend to _____

_____

_____

- When you are angry, you tend to _____

_____

_____

- When was our last argument? _____

_____

_____

- What was the problem? _____

_____

- How did we resolve it? _____

_____

FIGHTING FAIR

To presume that you will not argue after you are married is idealistic; it simply is not true. You will argue. Many marital therapists would say that a good conflict is often healthy because it promotes dialogue (couples *talk* with one another) and good communication. For some the experience of conflict in a prior marriage or relationship can make them hesitant to disclose their feelings and hurts, but they must take the risk and argue at times.

However, if arguments are to be fair and fruitful, they should follow certain ground rules. The object of an argument is to solve a problem, not to destroy the other person. Although to avoid conflict at all costs is unhealthy and stifling, to argue without certain positive guidelines can be destructive and disheartening. Here are a few tips.

Ground Rules

- Listen to your partner. Give each other the opportunity to speak and don't dominate the discussion.

- Stick to the issues at hand. Don't dredge up past hurts or problems, whether real or perceived.

- Never refer to your partner's former marriage in anger.

- Always complete the argument. To walk away angry or postpone the discussion indefinitely can cause more problems.

- Don't sling mud and arrows. Avoid name-calling. Use of phrases such as "stupid jerk," "fat slob," "drunken bum," or "lazy lump" only serves to hurt and incite more anger.

- Never threaten to withdraw love or sex.

- Don't use the "silent treatment." Nothing gets solved this way.

- When you are wrong, admit it.

- Don't make a scene. Never deliberately embarrass each other or others by arguing in front of other family members or in public. Keep your arguments private.

- Make up and mean it. Don't be bitter or carry a grudge.

Look over the behaviors listed below that are often used to express or respond to anger or negative feelings. In each case, check if it characterizes you, your new partner, or your former spouse(s), if any.

	ME	YOU	FORMER SPOUSE #1	FORMER SPOUSE #2
Silence				
Blaming				
Yelling				
Pouting				
Sarcasm				
Avoidance				
Appeasement				
Crying				
Threatening				
Physical Violence				

Remember: Differences of opinion, when brought to the forefront in a positive, careful manner, can help you grow. Don't argue to hurt and never go to sleep angry. Always call forth the core love you have for your partner and say goodnight with love in your heart.

To get in touch with your feelings and the manner in which you argue, answer the following questions and share your responses with your partner.

- When I get angry, I tend to _____

_____

_____

- When you are angry, you tend to _____

_____

_____

- When was our last argument? _____

_____

_____

- What was the problem? _____

_____

- How did we resolve it? _____

_____

16

SEX AND SEXUALITY

The more open and honest you and your partner are about your feelings and attitudes toward sex, the more fulfilling your overall relationship will be. Granted, sex is not the easiest subject to discuss openly—primarily because almost everyone experiences some anxiety when trying to verbalize feelings about sex. Although a natural aspect of human nature, sex is not simple: it involves roles, gender, physiology, emotions, and even a bit of mystery. No one has all the right answers, so you need not be experienced to be able to discuss sex—just be open to discussion and willing to listen.

To engage in open dialogue about sex, you must first understand yourself as a sexual being; that is, what has influenced you? How do you feel about sex? How do you feel about your partner sexually?

The questions in this exercise are designed to assist you in an honest appraisal of your sexual self. Jot down your responses and share them with your partner. Then *listen* to each other.

Questions

- Do you think that sex is: fun, frightening, threatening, satisfying, holy, expressive of your relationship, other? Give two descriptions that characterize your feelings about sex. _____

    _____

- What are your feelings about your body? _____

    _____

- What are your needs for affection? _____

    _____

- How affectionate are you? _____

    _____

- How comfortable are you when you touch and are touched? _____

    _____

- What events and attitudes from your past—especially any previous relationships—have influenced your sexual behaviors and attitudes? _____

    _____

- What memories or hang-ups (if any) must you work through to become comfortable and confident with your sexuality? _____

    _____

- Do you find anything offensive or vulgar about sex? _____

    _____

17

- What do you need most from your sexual relationship? _____
  _____

- As a sexual partner, a woman should _____
  _____

- As a sexual partner, a man should _____
  _____

- What circumstances do you find most exciting sexually? _____
  _____

- When would you not want to have sex? _____
  _____

- Do you find any specific acts immoral (improper) in marriage? Do you have any hesitations or reservations about sex? _____
  _____

- What worries you about sex in your marriage? _____
  _____

- What do your think your marital sex life will be like in ten years? _____
  _____

- What do you find physically attractive about your future spouse? _____
  _____

- What do you think your future spouse finds physically attractive about you? _____
  _____

SEX AND SEXUALITY

The more open and honest you and your partner are about your feelings and attitudes toward sex, the more fulfilling your overall relationship will be. Granted, sex is not the easiest subject to discuss openly—primarily because almost everyone experiences some anxiety when trying to verbalize feelings about sex. Although a natural aspect of human nature, sex is not simple: it involves roles, gender, physiology, emotions, and even a bit of mystery. No one has all the right answers, so you need not be experienced to be able to discuss sex—just be open to discussion and willing to listen.

To engage in open dialogue about sex, you must first understand yourself as a sexual being; that is, what has influenced you? How do you feel about sex? How do you feel about your partner sexually?

The questions in this exercise are designed to assist you in an honest appraisal of your sexual self. Jot down your responses and share them with your partner. Then *listen* to each other.

Questions

- Do you think that sex is: fun, frightening, threatening, satisfying, holy, expressive of your relationship, other? Give two descriptions that characterize your feelings about sex. _____

_____

- What are your feelings about your body? _____

_____

- What are your needs for affection? _____

_____

- How affectionate are you? _____

_____

- How comfortable are you when you touch and are touched? _____

_____

- What events and attitudes from your past—especially any previous relationships—have influenced your sexual behaviors and attitudes? _____

_____

- What memories or hang-ups (if any) must you work through to become comfortable and confident with your sexuality? _____

_____

- Do you find anything offensive or vulgar about sex? _____

_____

19

- What do you need most from your sexual relationship? _____
_____

- As a sexual partner, a woman should _____
_____

- As a sexual partner, a man should _____
_____

- What circumstances do you find most exciting sexually? _____
_____

- When would you not want to have sex? _____
_____

- Do you find any specific acts immoral (improper) in marriage? Do you have any hesitations or reservations about sex? _____
_____

- What worries you about sex in your marriage? _____
_____

- What do your think your marital sex life will be like in ten years? _____
_____

- What do you find physically attractive about your future spouse? _____
_____

- What do you think your future spouse finds physically attractive about you? ____
_____

KNOWING THE TERRITORY

It is especially important for couples entering a remarriage situation to be totally aware of each other's present financial situation before making their financial arrangements as a couple. The wisest course is for each of you to lay out your financial picture as completely as possible *before* the wedding. Be as honest as you can—this is no time for hiding the "bad news." Don't forget to include all possible liabilities, assets and income from previous marriages. After you have each completed this exercise separately, exchange your sheets and discuss your financial situation openly and realistically.

Your Liabilities

	Monthly Payments (if applicable)	Total Still Owed (if applicable)	Payoff Date (if applicable)
Mortgage/Rent (including property taxes)	$ _____	$ _____	$ _____
Car Loan	$ _____	$ _____	$ _____
Other Installment Loans	$ _____	$ _____	$ _____
Lines of Credit	$ _____	$ _____	$ _____
Credit Cards	$ _____	$ _____	$ _____
Other Loans	$ _____	$ _____	$ _____
Personal	$ _____	$ _____	$ _____
College	$ _____	$ _____	$ _____
Business	$ _____	$ _____	$ _____
Insurance	$ _____	$ _____	$ _____
Car	$ _____	$ _____	$ _____
Life	$ _____	$ _____	$ _____
Home	$ _____	$ _____	$ _____
Health/Disability (if not withheld)	$ _____	$ _____	$ _____
Income Taxes (if not withheld)	$ _____	$ _____	$ _____
Back Taxes Owed	$ _____	$ _____	$ _____
Medical and Dental Bills	$ _____	$ _____	$ _____
Pension/Retirement Contribution (if not withheld)	$ _____	$ _____	$ _____
Child Care	$ _____	$ _____	$ _____
Tuition/College Savings	$ _____	$ _____	$ _____
Child Support or Alimony to Former Spouse	$ _____	$ _____	$ _____

Your Assets

	Present Estimated Value
Real Estate	$ _____
Cash Savings	$ _____
Certificates of Deposit	$ _____
Stocks and Bonds	$ _____
Pension / Retirement Accounts	$ _____
Cash Value Life Insurance	$ _____
Other Investments	$ _____
Cars	$ _____
Furniture, Artwork, Jewelry	$ _____
Expected Inheritance	$ _____
Other Assets	$ _____

Your Income

	Estimated Monthly Income
Salary (Take Home)	$ _____
Bonus	$ _____
Dividends and Interest	$ _____
Rental Income	$ _____
Trusts and Gifts	$ _____
Alimony	$ _____
Child Support	$ _____
Other Income	$ _____

A Clear Picture

If you've both been able to fill in most of the information requested, you should have a good view of your financial situation as you enter your marriage. Now discuss what this means:

- Will there be enough money to cover your combined liabilities?

- How can you best combine your assets?

- What debts can be eliminated prior to the wedding?

- How much will you be able to save from your combined incomes?

- Will obligations to spouses and children from previous marriages be able to be met?

22

KNOWING THE TERRITORY

It is especially important for couples entering a remarriage situation to be totally aware of each other's present financial situation before making their financial arrangements as a couple. The wisest course is for each of you to lay out your financial picture as completely as possible *before* the wedding. Be as honest as you can—this is no time for hiding the "bad news." Don't forget to include all possible liabilities, assets and income from previous marriages. After you have each completed this exercise separately, exchange your sheets and discuss your financial situation openly and realistically.

Your Liabilities

	Monthly Payments (if applicable)	Total Still Owed (if applicable)	Payoff Date (if applicable)
Mortgage/Rent (including property taxes)	$ _____	$ _____	$ _____
Car Loan	$ _____	$ _____	$ _____
Other Installment Loans	$ _____	$ _____	$ _____
Lines of Credit	$ _____	$ _____	$ _____
Credit Cards	$ _____	$ _____	$ _____
Other Loans	$ _____	$ _____	$ _____
Personal	$ _____	$ _____	$ _____
College	$ _____	$ _____	$ _____
Business	$ _____	$ _____	$ _____
Insurance	$ _____	$ _____	$ _____
Car	$ _____	$ _____	$ _____
Life	$ _____	$ _____	$ _____
Home	$ _____	$ _____	$ _____
Health/Disability (if not withheld)	$ _____	$ _____	$ _____
Income Taxes (if not withheld)	$ _____	$ _____	$ _____
Back Taxes Owed	$ _____	$ _____	$ _____
Medical and Dental Bills	$ _____	$ _____	$ _____
Pension/Retirement Contribution (if not withheld)	$ _____	$ _____	$ _____
Child Care	$ _____	$ _____	$ _____
Tuition/College Savings	$ _____	$ _____	$ _____
Child Support or Alimony to Former Spouse	$ _____	$ _____	$ _____

Your Assets

	Present Estimated Value
Real Estate	$ _____
Cash Savings	$ _____
Certificates of Deposit	$ _____
Stocks and Bonds	$ _____
Pension/Retirement Accounts	$ _____
Cash Value Life Insurance	$ _____
Other Investments	$ _____
Cars	$ _____
Furniture, Artwork, Jewelry	$ _____
Expected Inheritance	$ _____
Other Assets	$ _____

Your Income

	Estimated Monthly Income
Salary (Take Home)	$ _____
Bonus	$ _____
Dividends and Interest	$ _____
Rental Income	$ _____
Trusts and Gifts	$ _____
Alimony	$ _____
Child Support	$ _____
Other Income	$ _____

A Clear Picture

If you've both been able to fill in most of the information requested, you should have a good view of your financial situation as you enter your marriage. Now discuss what this means:

- Will there be enough money to cover your combined liabilities?

- How can you best combine your assets?

- What debts can be eliminated prior to the wedding?

- How much will you be able to save from your combined incomes?

- Will obligations to spouses and children from previous marriages be able to be met?

IN-LAWS OR OUT-LAWS?

This exercise is designed to surface any anxiety either of you might have about the involvement of your families of origin in your marriage. The following statements will help you clarify both your understanding of situations and your concerns about them. Equally important, they will clarify any misunderstandings you might have about your partner's reactions to both families.

Remember: there is often a big difference between how you or your partner *think* (rationally, intellectually) about something and whether or not you are *bothered* (emotionally, on a feeling basis) about it. You may *think* something is true and yet not be *bothered* (apprehensive, nervous, worried, uptight) about it, or you may *feel* concerned about something even if you have no evidence that it is true.

First, mark the left side of the list under each category—**A, I Think; B, Bothers Me**—with your own reactions. Circle one dot under either Yes, No or Not Sure for each statement under each column. Remember: the first column is what you *think* to be the case, the second is how you truly *feel* about the situation.

When you have finished the entire list regarding your own reactions, go back and *re-read* each statement from what you believe is your partner's point of view. Then mark the right side of the list under each category—**C, You Think; D, Bothers You**—with how you believe your partner will respond. Circle one dot under either Yes, No or Not Sure for each statement under each column.

A			B				C			D		
I Think			**Bothers Me**				**You Think**			**Bothers You**		
Yes	No	Not Sure	Yes	No	Not Sure		Yes	No	Not Sure	Yes	No	Not Sure
•	•	•	•	•	•	1. One or both of our families of origin do not support our decision to marry.	•	•	•	•	•	•
•	•	•	•	•	•	2. My family does not accept you.	•	•	•	•	•	•
•	•	•	•	•	•	3. Your family does not accept me.	•	•	•	•	•	•
•	•	•	•	•	•	4. We will have difficulties in our marriage because our families of origin are of significantly different social, religious or economic backgrounds.	•	•	•	•	•	•
•	•	•	•	•	•	5. One or both of our families of origin will interfere in our marital relationship.	•	•	•	•	•	•
•	•	•	•	•	•	6. One or both of our families of origin will interfere in our decisions on running our household or raising our children.	•	•	•	•	•	•
•	•	•	•	•	•	7. One or both of us is unwilling to discuss our role in caring for our parents or other relative in their old age or illness.	•	•	•	•	•	•
•	•	•	•	•	•	8. Our own family will be affected by our having to care for one or more of our parents or other relative in their old age or illness.	•	•	•	•	•	•

Hold these sheets side by side and share with each other the results by comparing the answers each of you gave for A and B with those your partner gave for C and D.

If you differ on your perception of your relationships with your two families of origin (what you *think* is the situation), you need to discuss these items openly and honestly and decide how you are going to determine what is truly the case.

If one of you has a definite concern on a specific issue or if you gave different answers regarding one another's concerns (what you *feel* about the situation), it means that there are anxieties which still exist regarding your families of origin with which you must still deal.

INTIMACY CHECKUP

As a couple preparing for a remarriage, you want to share all aspects of your lives. Below is a list of areas of intimacy in which couples can grow closer together. Rate how you think you are doing in each area and prioritize what areas you believe you need to work on. Then share the results.

In the left column, prioritize the areas of intimacy in the order that you feel are most important to you personally (1 = most important, 10 = least important).

In the right column, rate how strongly you feel each area of intimacy is present in your relationship right now (1 = not present, 2 = present to a small degree, 3 = present to a considerable degree, 4 = very strongly present).

Prioritize 1–10   **Rate 1–4**

____ **Emotional intimacy**—feeling close, able to share deeply thoughts, hopes, and desires. ____

____ **Intellectual intimacy**—sharing in the world of ideas, able to talk about current affairs, ____ literature, or any area of the human spirit.

____ **Sexual intimacy**—experiencing closeness and union through physical sharing. ____

____ **Recreational intimacy**—having fun together in activities of mutual interest, playing ____ and enjoying new adventures.

____ **Work intimacy**—sharing common tasks such as household jobs, yardwork, community service projects; being interested in the other person's daily work. ____

____ **Communication intimacy**—using good communication skills in clear, honest discussions. ____

____ **Aesthetic intimacy**—appreciating the performing, written and visual arts, seeing the ____ beauty in nature and the products of human effort.

____ **Crisis intimacy**—dealing together with issues ranging from the small and everyday to ____ the most difficult and troublesome.

____ **Commitment intimacy**—trusting each other based on faithfulness and togetherness. ____

____ **Conflict intimacy**—resolving differences in a constructive manner. ____

IN-LAWS OR OUT-LAWS?

This exercise is designed to surface any anxiety either of you might have about the involvement of your families of origin in your marriage. The following statements will help you clarify both your understanding of situations and your concerns about them. Equally important, they will clarify any misunderstandings you might have about your partner's reactions to both families.

Remember: there is often a big difference between how you or your partner *think* (rationally, intellectually) about something and whether or not you are *bothered* (emotionally, on a feeling basis) about it. You may *think* something is true and yet not be *bothered* (apprehensive, nervous, worried, uptight) about it, or you may *feel* concerned about something even if you have no evidence that it is true.

First, mark the left side of the list under each category—**A, I Think; B, Bothers Me**—with your own reactions. Circle one dot under either Yes, No or Not Sure for each statement under each column. Remember: the first column is what you *think* to be the case, the second is how you truly *feel* about the situation.

When you have finished the entire list regarding your own reactions, go back and *re-read* each statement from what you believe is your partner's point of view. Then mark the right side of the list under each category—**C, You Think; D, Bothers You**—with how you believe your partner will respond. Circle one dot under either Yes, No or Not Sure for each statement under each column.

A I Think			B Bothers Me				C You Think			D Bothers You		
Yes	No	Not Sure	Yes	No	Not Sure		Yes	No	Not Sure	Yes	No	Not Sure
•	•	•	•	•	•	1. One or both of our families of origin do not support our decision to marry.	•	•	•	•	•	•
•	•	•	•	•	•	2. My family does not accept you.	•	•	•	•	•	•
•	•	•	•	•	•	3. Your family does not accept me.	•	•	•	•	•	•
•	•	•	•	•	•	4. We will have difficulties in our marriage because our families of origin are of significantly different social, religious or economic backgrounds.	•	•	•	•	•	•
•	•	•	•	•	•	5. One or both of our families of origin will interfere in our marital relationship.	•	•	•	•	•	•
•	•	•	•	•	•	6. One or both of our families of origin will interfere in our decisions on running our household or raising our children.	•	•	•	•	•	•
•	•	•	•	•	•	7. One or both of us is unwilling to discuss our role in caring for our parents or other relative in their old age or illness.	•	•	•	•	•	•
•	•	•	•	•	•	8. Our own family will be affected by our having to care for one or more of our parents or other relative in their old age or illness.	•	•	•	•	•	•

Hold these sheets side by side and share with each other the results by comparing the answers each of you gave for A and B with those your partner gave for C and D.

If you differ on your perception of your relationships with your two families of origin (what you *think* is the situation), you need to discuss these items openly and honestly and decide how you are going to determine what is truly the case.

If one of you has a definite concern on a specific issue or if you gave different answers regarding one another's concerns (what you *feel* about the situation), it means that there are anxieties which still exist regarding your families of origin with which you must still deal.

INTIMACY CHECKUP

As a couple preparing for a remarriage, you want to share all aspects of your lives. Below is a list of areas of intimacy in which couples can grow closer together. Rate how you think you are doing in each area and prioritize what areas you believe you need to work on. Then share the results.

In the left column, prioritize the areas of intimacy in the order that you feel are most important to you personally (1 = most important, 10 = least important).

In the right column, rate how strongly you feel each area of intimacy is present in your relationship right now (1 = not present, 2 = present to a small degree, 3 = present to a considerable degree, 4 = very strongly present).

Prioritize 1–10   **Rate 1–4**

____ **Emotional intimacy**—feeling close, able to share deeply thoughts, hopes, and desires. ____

____ **Intellectual intimacy**—sharing in the world of ideas, able to talk about current affairs, ____
       literature, or any area of the human spirit.

____ **Sexual intimacy**—experiencing closeness and union through physical sharing. ____

____ **Recreational intimacy**—having fun together in activities of mutual interest, playing ____
       and enjoying new adventures.

____ **Work intimacy**—sharing common tasks such as household jobs, yardwork, commu- ____
       nity service projects; being interested in the other person's daily work.

____ **Communication intimacy**—using good communication skills in clear, honest discus- ____
       sions.

____ **Aesthetic intimacy**—appreciating the performing, written and visual arts, seeing the ____
       beauty in nature and the products of human effort.

____ **Crisis intimacy**—dealing together with issues ranging from the small and everyday to ____
       the most difficult and troublesome.

____ **Commitment intimacy**—trusting each other based on faithfulness and togetherness. ____

____ **Conflict intimacy**—resolving differences in a constructive manner. ____

NOW'S THE TIME

This exercise assumes that neither of you have children from a prior relationship but are open to having children in your marriage.

Problems in marriage arise as often from misunderstandings as from differences of opinion. This is never more true than over issues involving children.

The following is a quick and easy exercise to confirm that you both have the same understandings about having and raising children, even though these understandings will certainly grow and mature over the years. On issues like these, don't assume that you have reached accord unless you have specifically done so.

For each issue, answer these two questions:

- Have you discussed this matter to your satisfaction?
- Have you agreed upon an answer for the time being?

Circle one dot under either Yes, No or Not Sure for each issue under each column.

Have we discussed?				**Have we agreed upon?**		
Yes	No	Not Sure		Yes	No	Not Sure
•	•	•	Having children?	•	•	•
•	•	•	Whether we are prepared to be parents?	•	•	•
•	•	•	The number of children we want?	•	•	•
•	•	•	How—if at all—we will attempt to space our children's births?	•	•	•
•	•	•	When we would like to begin having children?	•	•	•
•	•	•	Not being able to have children of our own?	•	•	•
•	•	•	The possibility of adopting or fostering children?	•	•	•
•	•	•	The possibility of raising a handicapped child?	•	•	•
•	•	•	Our beliefs about the way to discipline children?	•	•	•
•	•	•	The future education of our children?	•	•	•
•	•	•	The religious upbringing of our children?	•	•	•

Then compare your responses. Where there is disagreement or where either of you have answered Not Sure, there is need for further discussion both before and after the wedding. These questions are too important to ignore. You might want to save this exercise and redo it each year on your anniversary, just to make sure you're both on the same wavelength regarding the development of your family.

ARE WE READY?

This exercise assumes that neither of you have children from a prior relationship but are open to having children in your marriage.

The questions raised in this exercise are designed to help you begin to think about how prepared you are to assume the roles of father and mother.

Working alone, complete each of the following statements about your future family. Write or print the answers clearly so your partner can read them. Try to use phrases or sentences in your responses.

Share the results with your partner and then discuss your answers. Focus on those issues about which you have important concerns or differences and discuss how you will resolve them.

Three important qualities I think I will have as a parent:

_____

_____

_____

My greatest concern about my ability to be a good parent:

_____

_____

_____

Three important qualities I think you will have as a parent:

_____

_____

_____

My greatest concern about your ability to be a good parent:

_____

_____

_____

The main attitudes and behaviors I want to cultivate in our children:

_____

_____

_____

How we can prepare ourselves for parenthood:

_____

_____

_____

Resources we can turn to for help in parenting:

_____

_____

_____

NOW'S THE TIME

This exercise assumes that neither of you have children from a prior relationship but are open to having children in your marriage.

Problems in marriage arise as often from misunderstandings as from differences of opinion. This is never more true than over issues involving children.

The following is a quick and easy exercise to confirm that you both have the same understandings about having and raising children, even though these understandings will certainly grow and mature over the years. On issues like these, don't assume that you have reached accord unless you have specifically done so.

For each issue, answer these two questions:

- Have you discussed this matter to your satisfaction?
- Have you agreed upon an answer for the time being?

Circle one dot under either Yes, No or Not Sure for each issue under each column.

Have we discussed?				Have we agreed upon?		
Yes	No	Not Sure		Yes	No	Not Sure
•	•	•	Having children?	•	•	•
•	•	•	Whether we are prepared to be parents?	•	•	•
•	•	•	The number of children we want?	•	•	•
•	•	•	How—if at all—we will attempt to space our children's births?	•	•	•
•	•	•	When we would like to begin having children?	•	•	•
•	•	•	Not being able to have children of our own?	•	•	•
•	•	•	The possibility of adopting or fostering children?	•	•	•
•	•	•	The possibility of raising a handicapped child?	•	•	•
•	•	•	Our beliefs about the way to discipline children?	•	•	•
•	•	•	The future education of our children?	•	•	•
•	•	•	The religious upbringing of our children?	•	•	•

Then compare your responses. Where there is disagreement or where either of you have answered Not Sure, there is need for further discussion both before and after the wedding. These questions are too important to ignore. You might want to save this exercise and redo it each year on your anniversary, just to make sure you're both on the same wavelength regarding the development of your family.

ARE WE READY?

This exercise assumes that neither of you have children from a prior relationship but are open to having children in your marriage.

The questions raised in this exercise are designed to help you begin to think about how prepared you are to assume the roles of father and mother.

Working alone, complete each of the following statements about your future family. Write or print the answers clearly so your partner can read them. Try to use phrases or sentences in your responses.

Share the results with your partner and then discuss your answers. Focus on those issues about which you have important concerns or differences and discuss how you will resolve them.

Three important qualities I think I will have as a parent:

_____

_____

_____

My greatest concern about my ability to be a good parent:

_____

_____

_____

Three important qualities I think you will have as a parent:

_____

_____

_____

My greatest concern about your ability to be a good parent:

_____

_____

_____

The main attitudes and behaviors I want to cultivate in our children:

_____

_____

_____

How we can prepare ourselves for parenthood:

_____

_____

_____

Resources we can turn to for help in parenting:

_____

_____

_____

(STEP)PARENTING: A SPECIAL GIFT

This exercise assumes that children will already be present in your marriage from one or both sides. Answer the questions whether you will be a stepparent, a parent or both.

Beginning a marriage with children already present entails many special joys and frustrations. Complete the following questions and then share your answers with your partner.

1. As a (step)parent my greatest strength will be _____
_____

2. To me, being a good (step)parent means _____
_____

3. The method of discipline I think is most effective is _____
_____

4. As a (step)parent, I would like my children to _____
_____

5. My greatest concern for our children is _____
_____

6. One area of change I would like in our new family is _____
_____

7. One thing I can't control in our new family is _____
_____

8. I would like to have my (step)children think of me as _____
_____

9. My three qualities that will help me be a good (step)parent:
_____
_____
_____

10. Your three qualities that will help you be a good (step)parent:
_____
_____
_____

GUIDELINES FOR STEPFAMILIES

1. Give your children plenty of time to get to know your future spouse.

2. If you are divorced, reassure your children that your new relationship will not diminish their relationship with you. To reinforce this, arrange to spend time alone with them.

3. If you are widowed, the children may need time and space to grieve their deceased parent.

4. Let the children know that the decision to remarry is your decision, not theirs.

5. If possible, you may want to begin your new stepfamily life in a new home or apartment.

6. Let the children know what they can call you. Generally first names for stepparents are preferred to "Mom" or "Dad."

7. You need to arrange private time to nourish your relationship as a couple. Your relationship is primary and may be a positive model for the children.

8. Allow your stepfamily relationships time to develop. Don't expect "instant love."

9. Plan family activities involving not only all family members together, but also the different groupings separately, e.g., stepparent/stepchild(ren), parent/child(ren), stepsiblings alone.

10. To help children feel more secure and deal with loyalty conflicts, avoid critical remarks about former spouses. You may want to let the children know you understand their loyalty to their natural parent.

11. Encourage the children to talk about their original families. Allow them to display pictures of their natural parent if they wish.

12. Try to create a stepparent role somewhat different from that of the natural parent(s).

13. Present a united front to the children. The couple's unity is vital to the functioning of the stepfamily.

14. As much as possible, the natural parent should continue to be the primary disciplinarian.

15. If adolescent or older children or stepchildren have previously been fairly independent, allow them to remain so within reason.

16. Within reason, try to treat the children and stepchildren with equal fairness.

17. Make arrangements for "visiting" or noncustodial children to have a special place reserved for their clothes, toys, etc. Give them a chore and try to include them in some of the family's activities.

18. Although the children may be aware of the couple's new sexual relationship, it may be necessary to minimize some of the sexual aspects of the household by keeping displays of affection to a minimum.

19. Don't try to buy your children's or stepchildren's approval or cooperation.

20. It is better not to try to adopt your stepchildren if their natural parent is still living.

21. Ask your parents to accept the stepchildren. Grandparents are very important to the unity of the stepfamily.

22. Flexibility is a must in the stepfamily structure because of the multitude of differences that exist.

23. Physical touching is very important. Hold children if they are young. Hug them if they are older.

24. Natural parents feel hurt, angry and resentful at times. They may wish their older children would hurry and move out. If you have these feelings as a stepparent, you are not "wicked." You are only human.

25. Do not *try* too hard. This may cause stronger resistance from the stepchildren.

From *New Love, New Life* (Houston, TX: Family Life Services, 1987). Used with permission. All rights reserved.

(STEP)PARENTING: A SPECIAL GIFT

This exercise assumes that children will already be present in your marriage from one or both sides. Answer the questions whether you will be a stepparent, a parent or both.

Beginning a marriage with children already present entails many special joys and frustrations. Complete the following questions and then share your answers with your partner.

1. As a (step)parent my greatest strength will be _____
_____

2. To me, being a good (step)parent means _____
_____

3. The method of discipline I think is most effective is _____
_____

4. As a (step)parent, I would like my children to _____
_____

5. My greatest concern for our children is _____
_____

6. One area of change I would like in our new family is _____
_____

7. One thing I can't control in our new family is _____
_____

8. I would like to have my (step)children think of me as _____
_____

9. My three qualities that will help me be a good (step)parent:
_____
_____
_____

10. Your three qualities that will help you be a good (step)parent:
_____
_____
_____

GUIDELINES FOR STEPFAMILIES

1. Give your children plenty of time to get to know your future spouse.

2. If you are divorced, reassure your children that your new relationship will not diminish their relationship with you. To reinforce this, arrange to spend time alone with them.

3. If you are widowed, the children may need time and space to grieve their deceased parent.

4. Let the children know that the decision to remarry is your decision, not theirs.

5. If possible, you may want to begin your new stepfamily life in a new home or apartment.

6. Let the children know what they can call you. Generally first names for stepparents are preferred to "Mom" or "Dad."

7. You need to arrange private time to nourish your relationship as a couple. Your relationship is primary and may be a positive model for the children.

8. Allow your stepfamily relationships time to develop. Don't expect "instant love."

9. Plan family activities involving not only all family members together, but also the different groupings separately, e.g., stepparent/stepchild(ren), parent/child(ren), stepsiblings alone.

10. To help children feel more secure and deal with loyalty conflicts, avoid critical remarks about former spouses. You may want to let the children know you understand their loyalty to their natural parent.

11. Encourage the children to talk about their original families. Allow them to display pictures of their natural parent if they wish.

12. Try to create a stepparent role somewhat different from that of the natural parent(s).

13. Present a united front to the children. The couple's unity is vital to the functioning of the stepfamily.

14. As much as possible, the natural parent should continue to be the primary disciplinarian.

15. If adolescent or older children or stepchildren have previously been fairly independent, allow them to remain so within reason.

16. Within reason, try to treat the children and stepchildren with equal fairness.

17. Make arrangements for "visiting" or noncustodial children to have a special place reserved for their clothes, toys, etc. Give them a chore and try to include them in some of the family's activities.

18. Although the children may be aware of the couple's new sexual relationship, it may be necessary to minimize some of the sexual aspects of the household by keeping displays of affection to a minimum.

19. Don't try to buy your children's or stepchildren's approval or cooperation.

20. It is better not to try to adopt your stepchildren if their natural parent is still living.

21. Ask your parents to accept the stepchildren. Grandparents are very important to the unity of the stepfamily.

22. Flexibility is a must in the stepfamily structure because of the multitude of differences that exist.

23. Physical touching is very important. Hold children if they are young. Hug them if they are older.

24. Natural parents feel hurt, angry and resentful at times. They may wish their older children would hurry and move out. If you have these feelings as a stepparent, you are not "wicked." You are only human.

25. Do not *try* too hard. This may cause stronger resistance from the stepchildren.

From *New Love, New Life* (Houston, TX: Family Life Services, 1987). Used with permission. All rights reserved.

SHARING THE FAITH VISION

Sharing religious attitudes, concerns and questions with one another prior to marriage can have a very important effect on your respect for and understanding of each other. Religious faith can bring strength to your marriage; shared religious beliefs can increase the strength of marital love and the marital relationship. Often these beliefs and practices have been shaken or strengthened by a prior marriage.

Before you share your religious beliefs and attitudes, it might be worthwhile to clarify your thoughts in writing by answering the questions below. Share your feelings as openly and as freely as you can. If any of your responses or your discussions with one another raise concerns, it might also be worthwhile to initiate discussions with your priest, minister or rabbi.

1. When I pray, I _____

_____

2. When I pray, I pray about _____

_____

3. One good religious experience I've had is _____

_____

_____

4. A bad experience of religion that has turned me off is _____

_____

_____

5. On a scale of 1–10 (10 being most religious), I would rate myself this religious: ____

6. How satisfied are you with the level of religious intensity indicated in question 5? _____

7. I hope to share my faith and beliefs with my future spouse by _____

_____

_____

8. My reasons for marrying in a religious ceremony are _____

_____

_____

9. My faith helps me in my life and marriage by _____

_____

_____

10. I contribute to the life of my church or synagogue by _____

_____

11. In terms of my marriage, I would like to ask God for _____

_____

_____

12. Some of my questions, doubts and confusions about religion are _____

_____

_____

13. *(If previously married:)* Through my past experience of marriage I felt that God was _____

_____

_____

14. *(If you are an interfaith couple:)* Sharing my faith with my partner will benefit our marriage by _____

_____

_____

_____

15. *(If you are an interfaith couple:)* Some potential religious questions that might create problems for us are

_____

_____

_____

SHARING THE FAITH VISION

Sharing religious attitudes, concerns and questions with one another prior to marriage can have a very important effect on your respect for and understanding of each other. Religious faith can bring strength to your marriage; shared religious beliefs can increase the strength of marital love and the marital relationship. Often these beliefs and practices have been shaken or strengthened by a prior marriage.

Before you share your religious beliefs and attitudes, it might be worthwhile to clarify your thoughts in writing by answering the questions below. Share your feelings as openly and as freely as you can. If any of your responses or your discussions with one another raise concerns, it might also be worthwhile to initiate discussions with your priest, minister or rabbi.

1. When I pray, I _____

_____

2. When I pray, I pray about _____

_____

3. One good religious experience I've had is _____

_____

_____

4. A bad experience of religion that has turned me off is _____

_____

_____

5. On a scale of 1–10 (10 being most religious), I would rate myself this religious: _____

6. How satisfied are you with the level of religious intensity indicated in question 5? _____

7. I hope to share my faith and beliefs with my future spouse by _____

_____

_____

8. My reasons for marrying in a religious ceremony are _____

_____

_____

9. My faith helps me in my life and marriage by _____

_____

_____

10. I contribute to the life of my church or synagogue by _____
_____

11. In terms of my marriage, I would like to ask God for _____
_____
_____

12. Some of my questions, doubts and confusions about religion are _____
_____
_____

13. *(If previously married:)* Through my past experience of marriage I felt that God was _____
_____
_____

14. *(If you are an interfaith couple:)* Sharing my faith with my partner will benefit our marriage by _____
_____
_____
_____

15. *(If you are an interfaith couple:)* Some potential religious questions that might create problems for us are
_____
_____
_____

DISCUSSION/CHALLENGE QUESTIONS

1. What are some of the issues that still need to be worked through from your own or your partner's prior relationships?

2. What convinces you that this relationship will be a lasting one?

3. When is it easiest for you to talk about your feelings? When is it the hardest? How does your partner help or hinder your doing so?

4. What issues in your relationship may never be resolved (for example, religion, ex-spouses, in-laws, children)? How will you deal with such questions?

5. Your spouse-to-be's family probably shows affection in different ways than your own. How do you see this affecting your relationship?

6. How does your self-image impact the way you interact with your partner?

7. How will your past experiences with money affect the way you spend and save in your marriage?

8. Do either of you have an "addictive" personality? How will you deal with this?

9. How should religious faith be practiced in your family?

10. Is your spirituality similar to or different from your partner's? What does that mean for your marriage and any children you have now and might have together in the future?

LIST OF RESOURCES

As you examine your relationship with your future spouse, you may find you need more information or insights. There are many good books about couple relationships, stepparenting and creating your new life together. Listed below are some suggestions that might be helpful.

For You As a Couple:

Thomas, John, S.J. *Beginning Your Marriage*. Chicago: ACTA Publications, 1987. Seventh edition.

Satir, Virginia. *The New Peoplemaking*. Palo Alto, California: Science and Behavior Books, 1988.

For You As a Family

Berman, Claire. *Making It As a Stepparent*. New York: Doubleday, 1980.

Bernstein, Anne. *Yours, Mine and Ours—How Families Change When Remarried Parents Have a Child Together*. New York: Charles Scribner's Sons, 1989.

Curran, Dolores. *Traits of a Healthy Family*. Minneapolis: Winston Press, 1982.

Curran, Dolores. *Stress and the Healthy Family*. San Francisco: Harper & Row, 1985.

Rosen, Mark Bruce. *Step-Fathering—Stepfather's Advice on Creating a New Family*. New York: Simon & Schuster, 1987.

Savage, Karen, and Patricia Adams. *The Good Stepmother—A Practical Guide*. New York: Crown Publishers, 1988.

Visher, Emily B., and John S. Visher. *Stepfamilies—Myths and Realities*. Seacaucus, N.J.: Citadel Press, 1979.

Visher, Emily B., and John S. Visher. *How to Win As a Stepfamily*. Chicago: Contemporary Books, 1982.

For Your Children:

Bonkowski, Sara. *Kids Are Nondivorceable: A Workbook for Divorced Parents and Their Children*. (Ages 6–11) Chicago: ACTA Publications, 1987.

Bonkowski, Sara. *Teens Are Nondivorceable: A Workbook for Divorced Parents and Their Children*. (Ages 12–18) Chicago: ACTA Publications, 1990.

Bradley, Buff. *Where Do I Belong?—A Kid's Guide to Stepfamilies*. New York: Addison-Wesley, 1982.

Burt, Mala Schuster, and Roger B. Burt. *What's Special about Our Stepfamily?—A Participation Book for Children*. New York: Doubleday, 1983.

Gardner, Richard. *The Boys and Girls Book about Stepfamilies*. New York: Bantam Books, 1982.

Getzoff, Ann, and Carolyn McClenahan. *Stepkids—A Survival Guide for Teenagers in Step-families*. New York: Walker and Company, 1984.

EVALUATION FORM

Our goal in this program is to provide the best program possible for couples who are remarrying. Will you please help us by completing this evaluation form and returning it to your lead couple or facilitator? Thank you for participating in this process.

1. The atmosphere of these sessions has been: (circle one)

   relaxed & informal   5   4   3   2   1   *stiff & formal*

   Any comments? _____

   _____

2. In general, the leaders appeared to be: (circle one)

   sincere   5   4   3   2   1   *artificial*

   Any comments? _____

   _____

3. I found the information in this program to be: (circle one)

   very valuable   5   4   3   2   1   *of little value*

   Any comments? _____

   _____

4. Based on the material presented, my understanding of remarriage has been: (circle one)

   broadened   5   4   3   2   1   *unchanged*

   Any comments? _____

   _____

5. Completing the exercises was: (circle one)

   helpful   5   4   3   2   1   *boring*

   Any comments? _____

   _____

6. Would you recommend this program to a friend? (circle one)

   definitely   5   4   3   2   1   *not at all*

   Any comments? _____

   _____

7. What did you like *most* about this program? _____
_____
_____
_____

8. What did you like *least* about this program? _____
_____
_____
_____

9. Identify and comment about the presentation you liked the *best*. (Remarriage: Wonderful and Difficult, Communicating Effectively, Becoming Intimate, Potential Problems, Family Blending, Trusting God) _____
_____
_____
_____

10. Identify and comment about the presentation you found the *worst*. _____
_____
_____
_____

11. How can we improve this program? _____
_____
_____
_____

12. Have you been married before? _____ For how long? _____
Do you have children from a previous marriage? _____ How many? _____

EVALUATION FORM

Our goal in this program is to provide the best program possible for couples who are remarrying. Will you please help us by completing this evaluation form and returning it to your lead couple or facilitator? Thank you for participating in this process.

1. The atmosphere of these sessions has been: (circle one)

   relaxed & informal   5   4   3   2   1   *stiff & formal*

   Any comments? _____

   _____

2. In general, the leaders appeared to be: (circle one)

   sincere   5   4   3   2   1   *artificial*

   Any comments? _____

   _____

3. I found the information in this program to be: (circle one)

   very valuable   5   4   3   2   1   *of little value*

   Any comments? _____

   _____

4. Based on the material presented, my understanding of remarriage has been: (circle one)

   broadened   5   4   3   2   1   *unchanged*

   Any comments? _____

   _____

5. Completing the exercises was: (circle one)

   helpful   5   4   3   2   1   *boring*

   Any comments? _____

   _____

6. Would you recommend this program to a friend? (circle one)

   definitely   5   4   3   2   1   *not at all*

   Any comments? _____

   _____

7. What did you like *most* about this program? _____
_____
_____
_____

8. What did you like *least* about this program? _____
_____
_____
_____

9. Identify and comment about the presentation you liked the *best*. (Remarriage: Wonderful and Difficult, Communicating Effectively, Becoming Intimate, Potential Problems, Family Blending, Trusting God) _____
_____
_____
_____

10. Identify and comment about the presentation you found the *worst*. _____
_____
_____
_____

11. How can we improve this program? _____
_____
_____
_____

12. Have you been married before? _____ For how long? _____
    Do you have children from a previous marriage? _____ How many? _____

PRAYER SERVICE

Leader

An agape is a love feast. It symbolizes Jesus' last supper and represents a meal in which we gather to express our love and union with one another. It is the natural expression of the bond of love established by Christ in the Eucharist. It is the human sharing among persons—a sharing of their joy which overflows and deepens. This simple, prayerful celebration (or variations of it) can be done in your own homes. Often it is the prayerful beginning of a family meal. According to the Acts of the Apostles, the early Christians gathered together and "broke bread in their houses, they took food with gladness and simplicity of heart, praising God." Let us now begin our agape which for us will be the celebration of the end of our program with the following song.

Beginning Song

All

In union with Jesus Christ, we praise You, God our Father. We recognize that our love and union is a reflection of Your own redemptive love for all Your creatures. Lord, God, bless us as we gather to share our joy and ourselves. Let this agape be a symbol of our lives for one another through Christ, our Lord. Amen.

First Reading: 1 Cor. 13: 1–13

If I speak in human and angelic tongues but do not have love, I am a resounding gong or a clashing cymbal. And if I have the gift of prophecy and comprehend all mysteries and all knowledge; if I have all faith so as to move mountains, but do not have love, I am nothing. If I give away everything I own, and if I hand my body over so that I may boast but do not have love, I gain nothing.

Love is patient, love is kind. It is not jealous, love is not pompous, it is not inflated, it is not rude, it does not seek its own interests, it is not quick-tempered, it does not brood over injury, it does not rejoice over wrongdoing but rejoices with the truth. It bears all things, believes all things, hopes all things, endures all things.

Love never fails. If there are prophecies, they will be brought to nothing; if tongues, they will cease; if knowledge, it will be brought to nothing. For we know partially and we prophesy partially, but when the perfect comes, the partial will pass away. When I was a child, I used to talk as a child, think as a child, reason as a child; when I became a man, I put aside childish things. At present we see indistinctly, as in a mirror, but then face to face. At present I know partially; then I shall know fully, as I am fully known. So faith, hope, love remain, these three; but the greatest of these is love.

Second Reading: Mt. 22:34–40

When the Pharisees heard that he had silenced the Sadducees, they gathered together, and one of them, a scholar of the law, tested him by asking, "Teacher, which commandment in the law is the greatest?" He said to him, "You shall love the Lord, your God, with all your heart, with all your soul, and with all your mind. This is the greatest and the first commandment. The second is like it: You shall love your neighbor as yourself. The whole law and the prophets depend on these two commandments."

Brief Homily or Discussion

Kiss of Peace

Prayer of the Engaged Couples

God, our Father, we are here because we are people of love. We ask You to bless our love today and every day of our lives. Help us to be for each other a sign of Your perfect, unselfish, creative love. Help us to bring out all the best in each other, so that we may be truly creators of each other's best self—co-creators with You. Help us to heal and forgive, and to allow our partners to show us Your healing love when we need it.

As we prepare for a lifetime of commitment, a lifetime of love, be present with us. We invite You to be present in the day-to-day living out of our marriage covenant. Bless each couple here and give us all the grace that we need to begin our lives of truly happy and faithful married love. We ask this in the name of Jesus Your Son. Amen.

Breaking of Bread—Sharing of It with Others

Ending Song